How Smart Are You?

TEST YOUR IQ

Calculate Your IQ in Minutes

THOMAS J. CRAUGHWELL

BLACK DOG
& LEVENTHAL
PUBLISHERS
NEW YORK

Copyright © 2012 Black Dog & Leventhal Publishers, Inc.

Published by
Black Dog & Leventhal Publishers, Inc.
151 West 19th Street New York, NY 10011

Distributed by
Workman Publishing Company
225 Varick Street New York, NY 10014

Manufactured in China
Cover and interior design by Liz Dreisbach

ISBN-13: 978-1-57912-902-6
h g f e d
Library of Congress Cataloging-in-Publication Data available upon request

CONTENTS

INTRODUCTION

IQ is shorthand for "Intelligence Quotient." Since the first years of the twentieth century, tests have been given to children to determine if they were gifted, of average intelligence, or suffered from some type of disability and would do better in special education classes. The point of the IQ test was to assess a child's intellectual ability and predict his or her chances for success in the future. A child who scored in the gifted level would be put on track for college, while a child with average scores might be marked for one of the trades or office work.

Today, an IQ test is rarely given to children, but such tests are still given to adults as a way to measure their intellectual potential. Scoring has changed, too: Instead of measuring test results against a fixed standard, the scores of those who take an IQ test are compared to scores of other adults who have taken the test.

The standard scoring system for an IQ test is:

165 Genius
148–132 Gifted/Superior Intelligence
115 Higher Than Usual Intelligence
99 Average Intelligence
83 Low Average Intelligence
70 or below Very Low Intelligence

The fifty IQ quizzes in this book are intended for high school students and adults, and they are intended to be fun. Each chapter opens with more information about the IQ test and other tests of intelligence. Your scores will not reflect your actual intelligence, or predict how successful you will be in school or in your career. Furthermore, our IQ quizzes are brief; a real IQ test given by professionals is much more complicated and takes at least an hour to complete.

So enjoy these quizzes! On the one hand, don't get caught up in your score. But on the other hand, don't be surprised if the scores indicate that you're smarter than you thought you were.

CHAPTER 1

ODD SHAPE OUT

The Origins of the IQ Test

It all began with a simple case of family rivalry. Francis Galton (1822-1911) was one of those Victorian gentlemen who seemed able to do anything: he was a explorer, geographer, inventor, anthropologist, meteorologist, statistician, and even dabbled in what was then the new science of genetics. Yet Galton was a nobody compared to his famous cousin, Charles Darwin. Eager to grab his own share of the spotlight, Galton developed a theory that human intelligence was genetic, in other words, that it was inherited—intelligent parents were likely to have intelligent children. Furthermore, Galton believed that intelligence could be measured, thereby predicting how successful a child was likely to be in school.

Unfortunately, Galton's system of measurement focused on physical attributes such as reaction time and skin sensitivity rather than cognitive skills, and of course skin sensitivity does not predict whether a child is college material. Galton's method was rejected.

In France, the French government asked psychologist Alfred Binet (1857-1911) to develop a test that would measure a child's intelligence. France had just passed a law requiring all children to attend school, and there was widespread interest in learning which children were especially promising and which would require special assistance. Working with a colleague, Theodore Simon, Binet designed a test that had nothing to do with a typical school curriculum. Instead, Binet and Simon posed questions that revealed information about a child's attention span, recall capability, and problem solving skills. The Binet-Simon method was the first IQ test.

The test was studied in the United States by Lewis Terman, a psychologist at the University of Stanford. He tweaked the Binet-Simon test, creating in 1916 the Stanford-Binet Intelligence Scale. The Stanford test's most significant contribution was the intelligence quotient score. Terman's formula was to divide the child's mental age, or skills, with its chronological age, then multiply the result by 100. So, a child with a mental age or skills of a 12 year old and the chronological age of 10 would have an IQ score of 120.

In the early part of the 20th century the Stanford-Binet IQ test was used by the U.S. government to assess the intelligence of army recruits and even to screen immigrants when they arrived on Ellis Island.

✏️ Shape Analogies

1 Examine the shapes and identify the one that is least like the others.

(a) (b) (c) (d) (e)

2 Examine the shapes and identify the one that is least like the others.

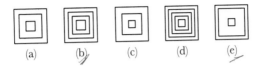

(a) (b) (c) (d) (e)

3 Examine the shapes and identify the one that is least like the others.

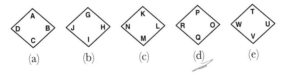

(a) (b) (c) (d) (e)

4 Examine the shapes and identify the one that is least like the others.

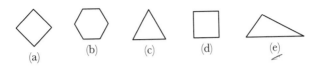

(a) (b) (c) (d) (e)

5 Examine the shapes and identify the one that is least like the others.

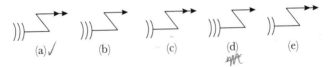

(a) (b) (c) (d) (e)

6 Cards 1 through 6 follow a pattern. Which card is next in the sequence?

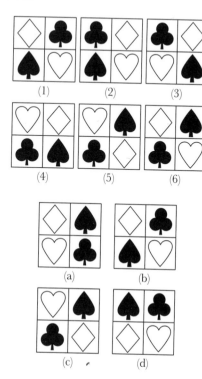

(1)   (2)   (3)

(4)   (5)   (6)

(a)   (b)

(c)   (d)

7 Examine the shapes and identify the one that is least like the others.

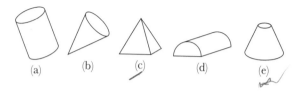

(a)   (b)   (c)   (d)   (e)

8 Which shape is next in the sequence?

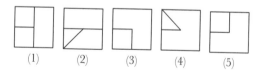

(1)   (2)   (3)   (4)   (5)

Choose from

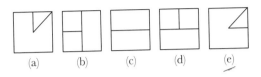

(a)   (b)   (c)   (d)   (e)

9 Which shape is next in the sequence?

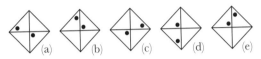

(a)   (b)   (c)   (d)   (e)

Choose from

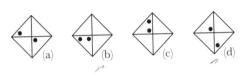

(a)   (b)   (c)   (d)

10 Examine the shapes and identify the one that is least like the others.

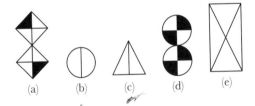

(a)   (b)   (c)   (d)   (e)

A N S W E R S ·

① B. In all the other shapes, the inside figure is a smaller version of the outside figure.

② B. It is the only figure with an even number of squares. All the others have an odd number.

③ D. It is the only diamond that does not have letters running in alphabetical order from the top and moving clockwise.

√ ④ E. It is the only shape in the series that is not symmetrical.

√ ⑤ A. It is the only figure in the series that does not have a twin.

⑥ B. In figure 2 the top two squares from figure 1 are transposed. In figure 3 the bottom two squares are transposed. In figure 4 the two vertical squares on the left are transposed. In figure 5 the two vertical squares on the right are transposed. In figure 6 the top left square and the bottom right square have been transposed. Therefore, in the next figure in the sequence, the top square on the right will be transposed with the bottom square on the left.

⑦ C. Figure C is made only with straight lines. All the other figures are made with straight lines and curves.

⑧ E. There are two moving lines in these figures: One moves 90 degrees each time, the other moves 45 degrees.

⑨ B. The dot at the outside of the figure moves clockwise, first one triangle, then two triangles, then three triangles, etc. The dot inside the figure moves counterclockwise, first one triangle, then two triangles, then three triangles, etc.

⑩ C. All the other figures will look exactly the same when turned upside down.

SCORING ·

Award 16.5 points for each correct answer.

165 Genius
148–132 Gifted/Superior Intelligence
115 Higher Than Usual Intelligence

99 Average Intelligence
83 Low Average Intelligence
70 or below Very Low Intelligence

More Shape Analogies

1 Select the figure that best completes the analogy.

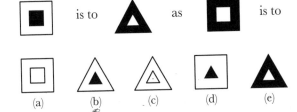

2 Select the figure that best completes the analogy.

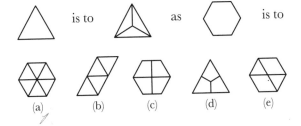

3 Select the figure that best completes the analogy.

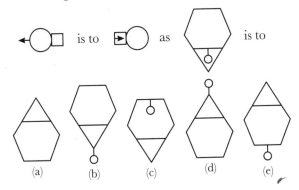

④ Select the figure that best completes the analogy.

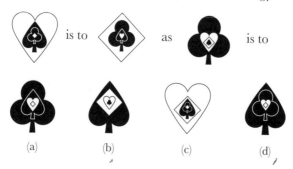

(a)   (b)   (c)   (d)

⑤ Select the figure that best completes the analogy.

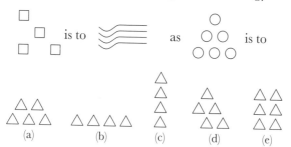

(a)   (b)   (c)   (d)   (e)

⑥ Select the figure that best completes the analogy.

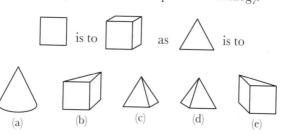

(a)   (b)   (c)   (d)   (e)

7 From the 5 figures below, choose the shape that best completes the analogy

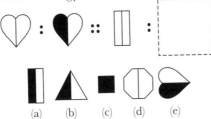

(a)   (b)   (c)   (d)   (e)

8 From the 5 figures below, choose the shape that best completes the analogy

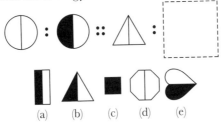

(a)   (b)   (c)   (d)   (e)

9 From the 5 figures below, choose the shape that best completes the analogy

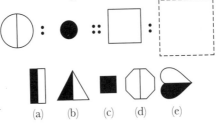

(a)   (b)   (c)   (d)   (e)

10 From the 5 figures below, choose the shape that best completes the analogy

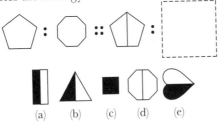

(a)   (b)   (c)   (d)   (e)

A N S W E R S ·

① B The shading of the inner and outer figures is reversed.

② A The hexagon is divided into six equal parts, just as the triangle is divided into three equal parts.

③ E The short lines in the figures are reversed.

④ B The sequence is this: The tiny center figure becomes the large outer figure; the next smallest inner figure becomes the next largest outer figure; the next smallest inner figure becomes the next largest outer figure; the largest outer figure becomes the tiny center figure.

⑤ E Four squares are to four lines as six balls are to six triangles.

⑥ C Like the cube, the pyramid shows its right side.

⑦ A The rectangle is shaded on the left side.

⑧ B The triangle is shaded on the left side.

⑨ C The small shaded square corresponds to the small shaded circle.

⑩ D The split hexagon corresponds to the split pentagon.

S C O R I N G ·

Award 16.5 points for each correct answer.

165 Genius
148–132 Gifted/Superior Intelligence
115 Higher Than Usual Intelligence
99 Average Intelligence
83 Low Average Intelligence
70 or below Very Low Intelligence

✏️ Pattern Recognition

Identify that letter or number that does not belong in each of the following series.

1
a. X
b. L
c. T
d. 7
e. 4

2
a. M
b. S
c. W
d. N
e. X

3
a. 4
b. Z
c. A
d. E
e. F

4
a. 2
b. O
c. C
d. Q
e. 8

5
a. F
b. Z
c. A
d. B
e. N

6
a. B
b. D
c. C
d. P
e. R

7
a. I
b. T
c. A
d. W
e. U

8
a. D
b. U
c. O
d. I
e. E

⑨ a. C

b. P

c. I

d. L

e. F

⑩ a. 6

b. 2

c. 8

d. 5

e. 4

ANSWERS ·

① e. 4. All the other characters are made with two lines.

② b. S. All the other characters contain angles.

③ d. E. All the other characters are made with three lines.

④ a. 2. All the other characters are based on round shapes.

⑤ c. A. All the other letters are consonants, A is a vowel.

⑥ c. C. All the other letters are made with a straight line and a curve.

⑦ e. U. The letters are in ascending order of the number of lines necessary to write them. U is made from a curve.

⑧ a. D. Four of the letters are vowels; D is a consonant.

⑨ b. P. When you count off the letters of the alphabet by three's, the other four letters are the third in the pattern.

⑩ d. 5. The other numbers can be divided by two.

SCORING ·

Award 16.5 points for each correct answer.

165 Genius

148–132 Gifted/Superior Intelligence

115 Higher Than Usual Intelligence
99 Average Intelligence
83 Low Average Intelligence
70 or below Very Low Intelligence

✏️ More Pattern Recognition

1 From the 6 figures below, identify the one that is significantly different from the other shapes.

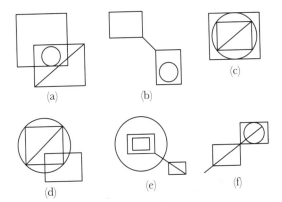

(a)   (b)   (c)

(d)   (e)   (f)

2 The shapes on the left hand form an incomplete analogy. From the 3 figures on the right, choose the shape that best completes the analogy.

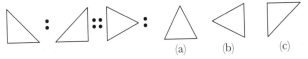

(a)   (b)   (c)

3 The shapes on the left hand form an incomplete analogy. From the 3 figures on the right, choose the shape that best completes the analogy.

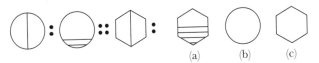

(a)   (b)   (c)

4 The shapes on the left hand form an incomplete analogy. From the 3 figures on the right, choose the shape that best completes the analogy.

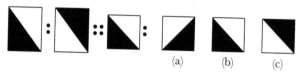

(a)   (b)   (c)

5 The shapes on the left hand form an incomplete analogy. From the 3 figures on the right, choose the shape that best completes the analogy.

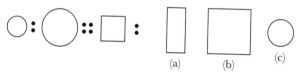

(a)   (b)   (c)

6 The shapes on the left hand form an incomplete analogy. From the 3 figures on the right, choose the shape that best completes the analogy.

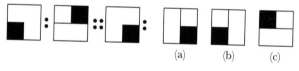

(a)   (b)   (c)

7 The shapes on the left hand form an incomplete analogy. From the 3 figures on the right, choose the shape that best completes the analogy.

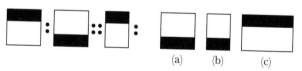

(a)   (b)   (c)

8 The shapes on the left hand form an incomplete analogy. From the 3 figures on the right, choose the shape that best completes the analogy.

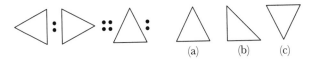

9 The shapes on the left hand form an incomplete analogy. From the 3 figures on the right, choose the shape that best completes the analogy.

10 The shapes on the left hand form an incomplete analogy. From the 3 figures on the right, choose the shape that best completes the analogy.

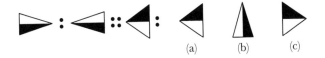

A N S W E R S ·

① B. It is the only figure that does not have two triangles.

② B. It is the mirror, or reverse, image of the equilateral triangle.

③ A. It has the horizontal bar pattern of the second circle.

④ C. It is the reverse image of the small square.

⑤ B. The larger square corresponds to the larger circle.

⑥ C. The shaded box flips on a diagonal and adds a line or tail.

⑦ B. It is equal in size to the first tall rectangle.

⑧ C. It is the opposite of the second triangle.

⑨ C. The two circles are the same size, so the two triangles must be the same size, too.

⑩ C. All the figures are mirror images of each other.

SCORING ·

Award 16.5 points for each correct answer.

165 Genius
148–132 Gifted/Superior Intelligence
115 Higher Than Usual Intelligence
99 Average Intelligence
83 Low Average Intelligence
70 or below Very Low Intelligence

CHAPTER 2

MATH
QUIZZES

The Wechsler
Intelligence Scales

In the 1930s an American psychologist, David Wechsler, studied human intelligence and defined it as an individual's capability "to act purposefully, to think rationally, and to deal effectively with his environment." He came to believe that the Stanford-Binet test was too limited; in an attempt to better measure intelligence over time, Wechsler created three IQ tests: the Wechsler Intelligence Scale for Children (WISC), the Wechsler Preschool and Primary Scale of Intelligence (WPPSI), and the Wechsler Adult Intelligence Scale (WAIS).

Wechsler rejected Stanford's method of scoring based on mental and chronological age. He developed a method in which test results were compared to the results of other test takers in the same age group. Wechsler found that 100 was an average score, and that two-thirds of children and adults who took his test scored between 85 and 115, which he said indicated normal intelligence.

David Wechsler's method became the standard scoring system for IQ tests in the second half of the 20th century, and is still used in IQ tests today.

✏️ Word Problems

1 On a recent test, Mary received the 11th highest and 11th lowest score in her class. How many students are in Mary's class?

A. 21   **C.** 11   **E.** 12

B. 22   **D.** 29

2 A sweater at a department store has been marked down 50 percent. For that same sweater to sell again at its original price, by what percentage must it be marked up?

A. 25%   **C.** 75%   **E.** 150%

B. 50%   **D.** 100%

3 In one day, a grocery store sold 360 kg of oranges. The store sold twice as many oranges in the afternoon as in the morning. How many kg of oranges were sold in the morning, and how many in the afternoon?

A. 80 kg in the morning, 280 kg in the afternoon

B. 90 kg in the morning, 270 kg in the afternoon

C. 120 kg in the morning, 240 kg in the afternoon

D. 100 kg in the morning, 260 kg in the afternoon

E. 140 kg in the morning, 220 kg in the afternoon

4 Morgan is 15 years old. He is 3 times older than his sister. At what age will he be twice as old as his sister?

A. 18   **C.** 24   **E.** 33

B. 21   **D.** 20

5 A car traveled 281 miles in 4 hours and 41 minutes. What was the car's average speed in miles per hour?

A. 75 miles per hour   **D.** 50 miles per hour

B. 60 miles per hour   **E.** 45 miles per hour

C. 55 miles per hour

6 Danny bought 20 baseball cards. Some cost 25 cents each, others cost 15 cents each. He spent $4.20 total. How many cards of each type did he buy?

A. 8 cards at 25 cents and 12 cards at 15 cents

B. 10 cards at 25 cents and 10 cards at 15 cents

C. 14 cards at 25 cents and 6 cards at 15 cents

D. 6 cards at 25 cents and 14 cards at 15 cents

E. 12 cards at 25 cents and 8 cards at 15 cents

7 A high school has 40 students in its senior class. Forty percent of the seniors are taking physics, 30 percent are taking chemistry, 10 percent are taking neither. How many seniors are taking neither physics nor chemistry?

A. 16 students   **C.** 18 students   **E.** 20 students

B. 17 students   **D.** 19 students

8 Two pumps working together can fill a water tank in 18 minutes. One pump works twice as fast as the other. If each pump worked alone, how long would it take to fill the water tank?

A. fast pump 20 minutes, slow pump 61 minutes

B. fast pump 23 minutes, slow pump 46 minutes

C. fast pump 27 minutes, slow pump 54 minutes

D. fast pump 30 minutes, slow pump 60 minutes

E. fast pump 33 minutes, slow pump 59 minutes

9 Ellie read two-thirds of a novel. The part she read was 90 pages longer than the unread portion of the novel. How many pages are in the book?

A. 300 pages   **C.** 295 pages   **E.** 250 pages

B. 270 pages   **D.** 287 pages

10 Taylor thought of a number, divided it by 5, then subtracted 154 and got 6. What is the number Taylor thought of?

A. 524   **C.** 400   **E.** 800

B. 774   **D.** 664

ANSWERS ·

① A. 23
② D. 100 percent
③ C. 120 kg in the morning, 240 kg in the afternoon
④ D. 20
⑤ B. 60 miles per hour
⑥ E. 12 cards at 25 cents and 8 cards at 15 cents
⑦ A. 16 students
⑧ C. fast pump 27 minutes, slow pump 54 minutes
⑨ B. 270 pages
⑩ E. 800

SCORING ·

Award 16.5 points for each correct answer.

165 Genius
148–132 Gifted/Superior Intelligence
115 Higher Than Usual Intelligence
99 Average Intelligence
83 Low Average Intelligence
70 or below Very Low Intelligence

Number Series

For each problem, identify the next number in the series.

1 5 6 10 12 20 23 40 44

A. 80   **C.** 24   **E.** 60

B. 66   **D.** 128

2 5 13 21 29 37 44

A. 53   **C.** 61   **E.** 54

B. 52   **D.** 51

3 2 5 10 17 26 37 50 65 82

A. 144   **C.** 88   **E.** 90

B. 101   **D.** 89

4 503 484 465 446 427 408

A. 398   **C.** 398   **E.** 389
B. 308   **D.** 399

5 737 774 811 848 885

A. 903   **C.** 922   **E.** 921
B. 907   **D.** 897

6 4 3 5 4 7 6 10 9 14 13 19 18

A. 21   **C.** 23   **E.** 25
B. 22   **D.** 24

7 17 51 153 459 1,377

A. 2,922   **C.** 3,759   **E.** 4,427
B. 3,123   **D.** 4,131

8 431 422 413 404 395

A. 386   **C.** 388   **E.** 385
B. 387   **D.** 389

9 291 293 586 588 1,176 1,178 2,356 2,358

A. 4,671   **C.** 4,716   **E.** 6,147
B. 4,167   **D.** 4,617

10 17 14 22 19 27 24 21 29 26 34 31

    A. 29   **C.** 41   **E.** 43

    B. 39   **D.** 46

A N S W E R S

① A. 80. The series solution is: Add 1, double the first number; add 2, double the third number; add 3, double the fifth number; add four, double the seventh number.

② B. 52. The series is created by adding 8.

③ B. 101. The series is created by adding odd numbers in numerical order beginning with 3. In other words, plus 3, plus 5, plus 7, plus 9, and so forth.

④ E. 389. The series is achieved by subtracting 19 from the previous number.

⑤ C. 922. The series is achieved by adding 37 to the previous number.

⑥ E. 25. The series is minus 1, plus 2; minus 1, plus 3; minus 1, plus 4; and so on.

⑦ D. 4,131. The number triples each time.

⑧ A. 386. Each number decreases by 9.

⑨ C. 4,716. The series pattern is plus 2, double the number.

⑩ B. 39. The pattern is minus 3, plus 8.

SCORING ·

Award 16.5 points for each correct answer.

165 Genius
148–132 Gifted/Superior Intelligence
115 Higher Than Usual Intelligence
99 Average Intelligence
83 Low Average Intelligence
70 or below Very Low Intelligence

➡ Missing Numbers

Identify the missing number in each series.

1 316 — 302 295 288 281

  A. 304   **C.** 301   **E.** 310
  B. 303   **D.** 309

2 6/24 12/48 18/72 24/96 30/120 36/ —

  A. 125   **C.** 143   **E.** 114
  B. 144   **D.** 126

3 39 78 117 195 312 507 —

  A. 819   **C.** 624   **E.** 818
  B. 737   **D.** 799

4 2 3 5 7 11 13 17 19 — 29 31

  A. 20   **C.** 22   **E.** 27
  B. 21   **D.** 23

⑤ 148 444 1,332 3,996 11,988 —

A. 23,000   **C.** 29,970   **E.** 35,964

B. 23,976   **D.** 33,102

⑥ 14,568 — 3,642 1,821 910.5 455.25

A. 12,366   **C.** 7,284   **E.** 9,324

B. 10,888   **D.** 8,675

⑦ — 246 239 232 225 218

A. 253   **C.** 255   **E.** 257

B. 254   **D.** 256

⑧ 655 663 — 679 687 695

A. 670   **C.** 675   **E.** 678

B. 671   **D.** 680

⑨ 926 936 931 941 936 946 — 951

A. 937   **C.** 939   **E.** 941

B. 938   **D.** 940

⑩ 31/93 47/141 52/156 66/198 74/222 89/ —

A. 231   **C.** 267   **E.** 266

B. 243   **D.** 255

ANSWERS ·

① D. 309. The series is achieved by subtracting 7 from the previous number.

② B. 144. The denominator is 4 times the numerator.

③ A. 819. The first number is doubled. Then each succeeding number is the sum of the previous 2 numbers.

④ D. 23. The numbers are all prime numbers, each of which can only be divided by 1 or by itself.

⑤ E. 35,964. The numbers triple.

⑥ C. 7284. Each number is half the number preceding it.

⑦ A. 253. Each number decreases by 7.

⑧ B. 671. Each number increases by 8.

⑨ E. 941. The pattern is plus 10, then minus 5.

⑩ C. 267. The denominator is 3 times the numerator.

SCORING ·

Award 16.5 points for each correct answer.

165 Genius
148–132 Gifted/Superior Intelligence
115 Higher Than Usual Intelligence
99 Average Intelligence
83 Low Average Intelligence
70 or below Very Low Intelligence

✏️ More Word Problems

1 It costs a DVD manufacturer X dollars per disc to make the first 1,000 discs of a DVD title. After the first 1,000, the cost drops to only one-third of X dollars. If X = $1.50, how much will it cost the manufacturer to produce 4,000 DVD discs?

A. $2,500 **C.** $3,500 **E.** $4,000

B. $3,000 **D.** $3,750

2 A train traveling at 60 mph enters a tunnel. The tunnel is 5 miles long. The train is 1 mile long. How many minutes will it take for the entire train to travel through the tunnel?

A. 10 minutes **C.** 8 minutes **E.** 6 minutes

B. 9 minutes **D.** 7 minutes

3 In a local election, the Republican candidate received one-and-a-half times as many votes as his Democratic challenger. The Democrat received one-third more votes than the Independent candidate. If the Independent received 900 votes, how many votes did the Republican receive?

A. 600 votes **C.** 1,500 votes **E.** 1,800 votes

B. 1,200 votes **D.** 1,700 votes

4 The full retail price of a CD is $8.95; 800 copies were sold. Sixty percent of the CDs were sold at 50 percent off the full retail price. Twenty percent were sold at 30 percent off the full retail price. The remainder were sold at the full retail price of $8.95. Rounding off to the nearest dollar amount, how much revenue was generated by sales of this CD?

A. $4,431   **C.** $4,213   **E.** $4,114

B. $4,582   **D.** $3,999

5 Hunter's workday begins at 8:45 a.m. and ends at 5:15 p.m. He is allowed 60 minutes for lunch and 30 minutes for coffee breaks. How many hours does Hunter work in five days?

A. 40 hours   **C.** 35 hours   **E.** 37 hours

B. 39 hours   **D.** 36 hours

6 A waiter in a restaurant presented a couple with a bill for their meal. The couple were charged $12.50 for appetizers, $28.55 for entrées, and $8.95 for desserts. The waiter added a 15 percent service charge to the bill. How much did the couple pay?

A. $56.25   **C.** $55.00   **E.** $51.50

B. $57.50   **D.** $52.75

7 The full retail price for a set of pencils is $1.80. As part of a back-to-school sale, the price has been discounted by 15 percent. What is the sale price for the package of pencils?

A. $1.53   **C.** $1.35   **E.** $1.60

B. $1.30   **D.** $1.49

8 In 1964, volleyball was included in the Olympic games. Seventy-three years before volleyball became an official Olympic sport, basketball was invented. In what year was basketball invented?

A. 1873   **C.** 1907   **E.** 1900

B. 1903   **D.** 1891

9 Scott and Lisa both collect baseball cards. Scott has 248 cards. Lisa has 75 cards more than Scott. How many cards are in Lisa's collection?

A. 299 cards   **C.** 323 cards   **E.** 335 cards

B. 301 cards   **D.** 275 cards

10 A fast food restaurant pays its employees $7.95 per hour Monday through Friday. Employees who work on Saturday or Sunday are paid $9.25 per hour. Starting on Monday, Ben worked seven hours per day for six consecutive days at the restaurant. How much did he earn in those six days?

A. $343   **C.** $303   **E.** $351

B. $299.25   **D.** $314.75

ANSWERS ·

① B. $3,000
② E. 6 minutes
③ E. 1,800 votes
④ B. $4,582
⑤ C. 35 hours
⑥ B. $57.50
⑦ A. $1.53
⑧ D. 1,891
⑨ C. 323 cards
⑩ A. $343

SCORING ·

Award 16.5 points for each correct answer.

165 Genius

148–132 Gifted/Superior Intelligence
115 Higher Than Usual Intelligence
99 Average Intelligence
83 Low Average Intelligence
70 or below Very Low Intelligence

Even More Word Problems

1 The number of chickens and pigs a farmer owns totals 8. If there are 26 legs in the barnyard, how many chickens are there, and how many pigs?

A. 1 chicken and 7 pigs
B. 2 chickens and 6 pigs
C. 4 chickens and 4 pigs
D. 5 chickens and 3 pigs
E. 3 chickens and 5 pigs

2 Michael, Carol, and Claire threw a party. They each invited 1 guest. Each of these guests invited 2 friends. Each of those friends invited 3 other friends. Assuming that everyone who was invited came to the party, how many people attended (including Michael, Carol, and Claire)?

A. 30 people
B. 33 people
C. 35 people
D. 37 people
E. 39 people

3 The population of the town of Woodbury grows every year. The first year 3 new families moved into town. The next year 8 families, the next year 13 families, and the year after that 18 families. Assuming that this pattern continues, in what year will 43 new families move into Woodbury?

A. the 8th year
B. the 9th year
C. the 11th year
D. the 12th year
E. the 13th year

4 A patron spends $11 on a movie ticket and popcorn. The ticket cost $5 more than the popcorn. How much was the movie ticket?

A. $5   **C.** $7   **E.** $9

B. $6   **D.** $8

5 The Makos softball team has 24 players. The Bears softball team has 27 players. The Mustangs football team has 18 fewer players than the 2 softball teams combined. How many players are on the Mustangs football team?

A. 33 players   **C.** 42 players   **E.** 19 players

B. 51 players   **D.** 29 players

6 Alex has $1,000 in his checking account. Saturday he deposited $250 in his account, and on Monday he withdrew $540. What is the balance in Alex's checking account?

A. $444   **C.** $710   **E.** $715

B. $625   **D.** $801

7 A Philadelphia parking garage charges $6 for the first hour and an additional $5 for each subsequent hour or part of an hour. If a tourist drops off her car at 6 p.m. and picks it up at 10:30 p.m., how much will she pay for parking?

A. $22   **C.** $24   **E.** $26

B. $23   **D.** $25

8 As a fund-raiser, a middle school class sold stationery. A box of notepaper cost $12; a box of note cards cost $8.

Total sales for the fund-raiser were $1,236. If the students sold 55 boxes of notepaper, how many boxes of notecards did they sell?

A. 68 boxes of note cards   **D.** 71 boxes of note cards

B. 72 boxes of note cards   **E.** 82 boxes of note cards

C. 69 boxes of note cards

9 Four teenage boys bought a used car for $1,250. They spent $575 on parts to repair it. The boys sold the repaired and rebuilt car for $4,605. The boys agreed to split up the profits from the sale equally. How much did each boy receive?

A. $1,825   **C.** $695   **E.** $780

B. $2,780   **D.** $525

10 Ten teams will participate in a softball tournament. Each team in the league must play every other team once and only once. How many games will be played in the tournament?

A. 45 games   **C.** 28 games   **E.** 10 games

B. 36 games   **D.** 21 games

ANSWERS ·

① E. 3 chickens and 5 pigs
② A. 30 people
③ B. the 9th year
④ D. $8
⑤ A. 33 players
⑥ C. $710
⑦ E. $26

⑧ B. 72 boxes of note cards
⑨ C. $695
⑩ A. 45 games

S C O R I N G ·

Award 16.5 points for each correct answer.

165 Genius
148–132 Gifted/Superior Intelligence
115 Higher Than Usual Intelligence
99 Average Intelligence
83 Low Average Intelligence
70 or below Very Low Intelligence

CHAPTER 3

SYNONYMS, ANTONYMS, OR NEITHER

The IQ Test Controversy

As the IQ test became a standard part of American society—it was used not only for school children but also by employers to gauge the suitability of prospective employees—some patterns began to emerge that some researchers as well as the-man-and-woman-in-the-street found unsettling. Blacks and Hispanics who took an IQ test tended to score lower than whites. The well-off tended to score better than the poor. And Asian Americans tended to score higher than any other racial group.

In the 1970s, critics blamed the designers of the IQ test for formulating questions that reflected white, middle class America. For example, a child was asked to complete the phrase "cup and…." "Saucer" was assumed to be the correct answer. But if the child grew up in a house where the family had no saucers, or did not use saucers, wouldn't the child's answer "table" be valid and equally correct?

As a result, psychologists, geneticists, social scientists, and other experts in the field of human intelligence began to debate whether environmental factors—where the test taker lived and how he or she was raised—had an impact on IQ scores. And if those factors did have an impact, to what extent? Although IQ tests continue to be given to children, the debate about the type of questions that appear on the test, and the accuracy of the scores rages on.

✏️ Synonyms, Antonyms, or Neither I

1 *Halcyon* and *limpid* are

   A. synonyms

   B. antonyms

   C. neither

2 *Narcissistic* and *vain* are

   A. synonyms

   B. antonyms

   C. neither

3 *Ravenous* and *blackbird* are

   A. synonyms

   B. antonyms

   C. neither

4 *Inglorious* and *disgraceful* are

   A. synonyms

   B. antonyms

   C. neither

5 *Pallid* and *ruddy* are

   A. synonyms

   B. antonyms

   C. neither

6 *Virile* and *virulent* are

   A. synonyms

   B. antonyms

   C. neither

7 *Affianced* and *engaged* are

   A. synonyms

   B. antonyms

   C. neither

8 *Effrontery* and *frontage* are

   A. synonyms

   B. antonyms

   C. neither

9 *Notable* and *significant* are

   A. synonyms

   B. antonyms

   C. neither

10 *Porous* and *impoverished* are

   A. synonyms

   B. antonyms

   C. neither

ANSWERS ·

① C. neither
② A. synonyms
③ C. neither
④ A. synonyms
⑤ B. antonyms

⑥ C. neither
⑦ A. synonyms
⑧ C. neither
⑨ A. synonyms
⑩ C. neither

SCORING ·

Award 16.5 points for each correct answer.

165 Genius
148–132 Gifted/Superior Intelligence
115 Higher Than Usual Intelligence
99 Average Intelligence
83 Low Average Intelligence
70 or below Very Low Intelligence

✏️ Synonyms, Antonyms, or Neither II

① *Hidebound* and *leather* are

A. synonyms

B. antonyms

C. neither

② *Morass* and *quagmire* are

A. synonyms

B. antonyms

C. neither

③ *Noisome* and *attractive* are

A. synonyms

B. antonyms

C. neither

④ *Vignette* and *vinegar* are

A. synonyms

B. antonyms

C. neither

5 *Bauble* and *treasure* are

A. synonyms

B. antonyms

C. neither

6 *Gigolo* and *flute* are

A. synonyms

B. antonyms

C. neither

7 *Didactic* and *moralizing* are

A. synonyms

B. antonyms

C. neither

8 *Harbinger* and *messenger* are

A. synonyms

B. antonyms

C. neither

9 *Nepotism* and *despotism* are

A. synonyms

B. antonyms

C. neither

10 *Nadir* and *climax* are

A. synonyms

B. antonyms

C. neither

ANSWERS

① C. neither
② A. synonyms
③ B. antonyms
④ C. neither
⑤ B. antonyms

⑥ C. neither
⑦ A. synonyms
⑧ A. synonyms
⑨ C. neither
⑩ B. antonyms

SCORING

Award 16.5 points for each correct answer.

165 Genius
148–132 Gifted/Superior Intelligence
115 Higher Than Usual Intelligence
99 Average Intelligence

83 Low Average Intelligence
70 or below Very Low Intelligence

✏️ Synonyms, Antonyms, or Neither III

1 *Bane* and *nuisance* are

A. synonyms

B. antonyms

C. neither

2 *Lachrymose* and *jolly* are

A. synonyms

B. antonyms

C. neither

3 *Polarize* and *divide* are

A. synonyms

B. antonyms

C. neither

4 *Vassal* and *flower pot* are

A. synonyms

B. antonyms

C. neither

5 *Clique* and *faction* are

A. synonyms

B. antonyms

C. neither

6 *Virtuoso* and *saint* are

A. synonyms

B. antonyms

C. neither

7 *Forte* and *weakness* are

A. synonyms

B. antonyms

C. neither

8 *Mountebank* and *fraud* are

A. synonyms

B. antonyms

C. neither

9 *Risible* and *solemn* are

A. synonyms

B. antonyms

C. neither

10 *Élan* and *styleless* are

A. synonyms

B. antonyms

C. neither

A N S W E R S ·

① A. synonyms
② B. antonyms
③ A. synonyms
④ C. neither
⑤ A. synonyms

⑥ C. neither
⑦ B. antonyms
⑧ A. synonyms
⑨ B. antonyms
⑩ B. antonyms

S C O R I N G ·

Award 16.5 points for each correct answer.

165 Genius
148–132 Gifted/Superior Intelligence
115 Higher Than Usual Intelligence
99 Average Intelligence
83 Low Average Intelligence
70 or below Very Low Intelligence

✏️ Synonyms, Antonyms, or Neither IV

❶ *Immure* and *liberate* are

A. synonyms

B. antonyms

C. neither

❷ *Diaphanous* and *sheer* are

A. synonyms

B. antonyms

C. neither

❸ *Maladroit* and *skillful* are

A. synonyms

B. antonyms

C. neither

❹ *Salubrious* and *cheesy* are

A. synonyms

B. antonyms

C. neither

5 *Traumatic* and *joyous* are

    A. synonyms

    B. antonyms

    C. neither

6 *Impulsive* and *compound* are

    A. synonyms

    B. antonyms

    C. neither

7 *Portentous* and *significant* are

    A. synonyms

    B. antonyms

    C. neither

8 *Fastidious* and *sloppy* are

    A. synonyms

    B. antonyms

    C. neither

9 *Nemesis* and *archenemy* are

    A. synonyms

    B. antonyms

    C. neither

10 *Gargantuan* and *mouthwash* are

    A. synonyms

    B. antonyms

    C. neither

ANSWERS ·

① B. antonyms

② A. synonyms

③ B. antonyms

④ C. neither

⑤ B. antonyms

⑥ C. neither

⑦ A. synonyms

⑧ B. antonyms

⑨ A. synonyms

⑩ C. neither

SCORING ·

Award 16.5 points for each correct answer.

165 Genius

148–132 Gifted/Superior Intelligence

115 Higher Than Usual Intelligence
99 Average Intelligence
83 Low Average Intelligence
70 or below Very Low Intelligence

Synonyms, Antonyms, or Neither V

1 *Heyday* and *harvest* are

   A. synonyms

   B. antonyms

   C. neither

2 *Prolix* and *long-winded* are

   A. synonyms

   B. antonyms

   C. neither

3 *Kudos* and *congratulations* are

   A. synonyms

   B. antonyms

   C. neither

4 *Fortnight* and *barricade* are

   A. synonyms

   B. antonyms

   C. neither

5 *Acumen* and *foolishness* are

   A. synonyms

   B. antonyms

   C. neither

6 *Lackey* and *master* are

   A. synonyms

   B. antonyms

   C. neither

7 *Liaison* and *love affair* are

   A. synonyms

   B. antonyms

   C. neither

8 *Apocryphal* and *fictional* are

   A. synonyms

   B. antonyms

   C. neither

9 *Fawning* and *haughty* are

    A. synonyms

    B. antonyms

    C. neither

10 *Patrician* and *aristocrat* are

    A. synonyms

    B. antonyms

    C. neither

ANSWERS

① C. neither
② A. synonyms
③ A. synonyms
④ C. neither
⑤ B. antonyms

⑥ B. antonyms
⑦ A. synonyms
⑧ A. synonyms
⑨ B. antonyms
⑩ A. synonyms

SCORING

Award 16.5 points for each correct answer.

    165 Genius
    148–132 Gifted/Superior Intelligence
    115 Higher Than Usual Intelligence
    99 Average Intelligence
    83 Low Average Intelligence
    70 or below Very Low Intelligence

CHAPTER 4

TEST YOUR VOCABULARY

IQ Scores of People in Hisstory

What was Galileo's IQ score? Or Abraham Lincoln's? Or the ancient philosopher and mathematician Hypatia's? It sounds like a trick question, because the IQ test did not exist when these famous people were alive. Nonetheless, in the 1920s Catherine Cox Miles, an American psychologist, began to study the developmental histories of 100 geniuses. She identified 67 character traits that became her basis for calculating IQ.

In the 1990s, Tony Buzan, an English expert in intelligence and accelerated learning, confirmed Cox Miles' work, but added the IQs of several more genius to the list and in some cases gave new scores to the geniuses on Cox Miles' list. What follows is a sampling from Cox Miles' and Buzan's studies.

William Shakespeare 210 (Buzan)
Sir Isaac Newton 190 (Buzan 195)
Leonardo da Vinci 180 (Buzan 220)
Marie Curie 180 (Buzan)
George Friedrich Handel 170
Hypatia 170 (Buzan 210)
Galileo Galilei 165
Charlotte Bronte 165
Wolfgang Amadeus Mozart, 165
Albert Einstein 160 (205 Buzan)
Benjamin Franklin 160 (Buzan 185)
Thomas Jefferson, 160
Charles Darwin 153
George Eliot (Mary Ann Evans) 150 (Buzan 180)
Abraham Lincoln 150
George Washington 140
Ulysses S. Grant 130

✏️ Test Your Vocabulary I

1 Something said to be *toxic* is

    A. annoying

    B. poisonous

    C. noisy

    D. oily

    E. round

2 A *repast* is a(n)

    A. meal

    B. instant replay

    C. historical event

    D. nap

    E. repeating rifle

3 An *obstreperous* child is

    A. overweight

    B. suffering from strep throat

    C. defiant

    D. small for his or her age

    E. athletic

4 An *itinerant* person

    A. wanders from place to place

    B. has a short attention span

    C. is poorly educated

    D. asks for spare change

    E. can't hold a job

5 To take *umbrage* is to

    A. steal

    B. feel offended

    C. try a sample

    D. find a shady spot

    E. rest

6 A *hierarch* is a(n)

    A. skydiver

    B. bishop

    C. ancient alphabet

    D. bridge builder

    E. snob

7 Someone who is *bibulous*

    A. drinks too much alcohol

    B. drools

    C. likes lettuce

    D. acts foolishly

    E. is a bad dancer

8 A *fecund* field is

    A. rotting

    B. barren

    C. full of weeds

    D. overgrown

    E. fertile

⑨ To act with *aplomb* is to be

A. shy

B. loud

C. nervous

D. self-confident

E. self-conscious

⑩ A *misanthrope*

A. hates people

B. causes a sore throat

C. is a female antelope

D. is a mathematical equation

E. studies the stars

ANSWERS ·

① B. poisonous
② A. meal
③ C. defiant
④ A. wanders from place to place
⑤ B. feel offended

⑥ B. bishop
⑦ A. drinks too much alcohol
⑧ E. fertile
⑨ D. self-confident
⑩ A. hates people

SCORING ·

Award 16.5 points for each correct answer.

165 Genius
148–132 Gifted/Superior Intelligence
115 Higher Than Usual Intelligence
99 Average Intelligence
83 Low Average Intelligence
70 or below Very Low Intelligence

Test Your Vocabulary II

1 An *augury* is a(n)

A. stable

B. woodworking tool

C. prediction

D. renowned speaker

E. herb

2 To be *feckless* is to be

A. incompetent or lack initiative

B. without hair

C. unlucky

D. unfertile

C. dejected

3 Something described as *tawdry* is

A. immoral

B. broken

C. dry

D. cheap or gaudy

E. poor

4 A *boor* is a

A. wild pig

B. domestic male hog

C. person with no manners

D. small hole in fabric

E. South African colonist

5 To *stipulate* is

A. to sprinkle

B. to cover with dots

C. to drink too much

D. to be tardy

E. to specify

6 A fabric described as *diaphanous* is

A. birdlike

B. thin and transparent

C. feathery

D. dense

E. cumbersome

7 To have a *penchant* is

A. to have tendency or an inclination

B. to pretend

C. to write well

D. to think carefully

E. to dream

8 To *incise* is

   A. to dedicate a book to someone

   B. to tailor

   C. to sort clippings for a scrapbook

   D. to carve or cut into a surface, such as a stone

   E. to adorn with jewels

9 A *feint* is a

   A. swoon

   B. forgery

   C. lie

   D. masquerade

   E. pretend attack

10 To be *inured* is

   A. to be buried alive

   B. to be accustomed or hardened to suffering or pain

   C. to be covered by an insurance policy

   D. to suffer a serious injury

   E. to be falsely accused

ANSWERS

① C. prediction
② A. incompetent or lack initiative
③ D. cheap or gaudy
④ C. a person with no manners
⑤ E. to specify
⑥ B. thin and transparent
⑦ A. to have tendency or an inclination
⑧ D. to carve or cut into something, such as a stone
⑨ E. pretend attack
⑩ B. to be accustomed or hardened to suffering or pain

SCORING

Award 16.5 points for each correct answer.

165 Genius

148–132 Gifted/Superior Intelligence
115 Higher Than Usual Intelligence
99 Average Intelligence
83 Low Average Intelligence
70 or below Very Low Intelligence

Test Your Vocabulary III

1 A person described as *mettlesome* is

A. meddlesome

B. courageous

C. stubborn

D. stingy

E. handsome

2 To be *foppish* is

A. to be a thoughtless child

B. to be a cautious woman

C. to be a romantic girl

D. to be a wise elderly man or woman

E. to be a man overly concerned about fashionable clothing and accessories

3 A *gaffe* is a

A. type of gazelle

B. sharp metal hook

C. colloquial expression for a father

D. social blunder or mistake

E. type of garlic

4 To be an object of *opprobrium* is

A. to be admired

B. to be imitated

C. to be treated with scorn or contempt

D. to be treated as an equal

E. to be slow or dull-witted

5 To be *recumbent* is to

A. lie down

B. curtsy

C. sit upright

D. make a low bow

E. straddle a chair

6 To be *culpable* is

A. to be engaged to marry

B. to be guilty of some wrongdoing

C. to be romantically involved with someone else's spouse

D. to have artistic talent

E. to be sympathetic

7 Something described as *runic* is

A. falling down

B. fast or quick

C. ancient

D. misshaped

E. mysterious or magical

8 An ailment described as *chronic* is

A. incurable

B. persistent or long-lasting

C. fatal

D. imaginary

E. contagious

9 To be *discerning* is

A. to be perceptive

B. to be disrespectful

C. to be confused

D. to be careless

E. to be prejudiced

10 A person described as *churlish* is

A. short

B. portly

C. rude

D. immature

E. physically unattractive

ANSWERS ··

① A. interfering

② E. to be a man overly concerned about fashionable clothing and accessories

③ D. social blunder or mistake
④ C. to be an object of scorn or contempt
⑤ A. lie down
⑥ B. to be guilty of some wrongdoing
⑦ E. mysterious or magical
⑧ B. persistent or long-lasting
⑨ A. to be perceptive
⑩ C. rude

S C O R I N G ·

Award 16.5 points for each correct answer.

165 Genius
148–132 Gifted/Superior Intelligence
115 Higher Than Usual Intelligence
99 Average Intelligence
83 Low Average Intelligence
70 or below Very Low Intelligence

✏ Test Your Vocabulary IV

❶ A *demagogue* is a(n)

    A. advocate of democracy

    B. pompous schoolteacher

    C. sensitive audio system

    D. political leader who appeals to citizens' fears

    E. a community activist

❷ An *interregnum* is a(n)

    A. period between two reigns or governments

    B. imperial crown

    C. official attached to a monarch's court

    D. courtroom

    E. ambassador

3 A person said to possess *dexterity* is

A. right-handed

B. politically and socially conservative

C. skillful with his or her hands

D. unshakable in his or her opinions

E. a popular public speaker

4 A *raconteur* is a(n)

A. nocturnal animal

B. cat burglar

C. French chef

D. gangster

E. gifted storyteller

5 To be *solicitous* of another person is

A. to represent him or her in court

B. to request a favor

C. to beg for a hand-out

D. to be thoughtful and express concern

E. to be critical

6 To *coerce* others is

A. to insult or belittle them

B. to force them to do something they do not want to do

C. to demand payment of a debt

D. to cooperate with them

E. to praise them

7 Something described as *iniquitous* is

A. evil

B. left-handed

C. wise

D. nosy

E. out of balance

8 A *milliner*

A. grinds grain

B. mends clothes

C. grows millet

D. runs marathons

E. makes hats

9 Someone described
as *dapper* is

  A. friendly and outgoing

  B. young and handsome

  C. kind and generous

  D. neat and well-dressed

  E. polite and articulate

10 Something said to be
occluded is

  A. unable to see

  B. out of date and useless

  C. blocked from moving
forward

  D. difficult to understand

  E. thick with fog

ANSWERS

① D. political leader who appeals to citizens' fears
② A. period between two reigns of governments
③ C. skillful with his or her hands
④ E. gifted storyteller
⑤ D. to be thoughtful and express concern
⑥ B. to force them to do something they do not want to do
⑦ A. evil
⑧ E. makes hats
⑨ D. neat and well-dressed
⑩ C. blocked from moving forward

SCORING

Award 16.5 points for each correct answer.

165 Genius
148–132 Gifted/Superior Intelligence
115 Higher Than Usual Intelligence
99 Average Intelligence
83 Low Average Intelligence
70 or below Very Low Intelligence

✏️ Test Your Vocabulary V

1 To be *avaricious* is

   A. to strive for success

   B. to desire money

   C. to love birds

   D. to be generous

   E. to be excessively proud

2 A period or place described as *halcyon* is

   A. frighteningly unfamiliar

   B. mythical

   C. exotic

   D. aristocratic

   E. happy and peaceful

3 To be *testy* is

   A. to be good at taking tests

   B. to enjoy giving tests

   C. to be irritable

   D. to be reliable

   E. to be exact

4 Someone described as *maudlin* is

   A. ruddy-faced

   B. insincere

   C. fond of children

   D. sentimental to the point of weeping

   E. arrogant

5 A *cumbersome* object is

   A. orange in color

   B. fragrant and appealing

   C. bulky and hard to move or carry

   D. ideally situated

   E. off-putting

6 A *forward* person is

   A. proud and conceited

   B. presumptuous and bold

   C. ahead of his or her time

   D. thoughtful and considerate

   E. imaginative

7 A *fortnight* is a period of

A. fourteen days

B. forty days

C. four hours

D. fourteen minutes

E. forty years

8 To be *supine* is

A. to sip soup

B. to siphon liquid

C. to be late for supper

D. to bend over

E. to be flat on one's back

9 A *quisling* is a

A. teenage boy

B. knight on a quest

C. traitor

D. secret agent

E. test-taker

10 Someone described as *emaciated* is

A. unusually attractive

B. excessively, even dangerously thin

C. taller than average

D. freed from slavery

E. elderly and feeble

ANSWERS ·

① B. to desire money
② E. happy and peaceful
③ C. to be irritable
④ D. sentimental to the point of weeping
⑤ C. bulky and hard to move or carry
⑥ B. presumptuous and bold
⑦ A. two weeks or fourteen days
⑧ E. to be flat on one's back
⑨ C. a traitor
⑩ B. excessively, even dangerously thin

SCORING ·

Award 16.5 points for each correct answer.

165 Genius
148–132 Gifted/Superior Intelligence
115 Higher Than Usual Intelligence
99 Average Intelligence
83 Low Average Intelligence
70 or below Very Low Intelligence

CHAPTER 5

RECOGNIZING PATTERNS

IQ Scores of Famous Contemporary People

Just about everyone who was born in the second half of the 20th century took an IQ test, so it is much easier to learn their scores than the scores of people from the distant past.

Gary Kasparov, chess champion, 190
Bobby Fischer, chess champion, 187
Benjamin Netanyahu, prime minister of Israel, 180
Bill Gates, founder of Microsoft, 160
Stephen Hawking, physicist and author, 160
Reggie Jackson, professional baseball player, 160
Richard Nixon, former president of the United States, 143
Hillary Clinton, US secretary of state and former First Lady, 140

Bill Clinton, former US president, 137
George W. Bush, former US president, 125
Gerald Ford, former president of the United States, 121

✏ Recognizing Patterns I

In each of the following groups of words, select the word that is not like the others.

1 **A.** novel

   B. poem

   C. painting

   D. flower

   E. sculpture

2 **A.** radish

   B. tomato

   C. pear

   D. apple

   E. orange

3 **A.** shredder

   B. knife

   C. razor

   D. chainsaw

   E. grater

4 **A.** heron

   B. swan

   C. penguin

   D. duck

   E. goose

5 **A.** euro

   B. dollar

   C. diamond

   D. pound

   E. franc

6 **A.** bus

   B. cab

   C. train

   D. subway

   E. monorail

7 **A.** lion

   B. tiger

   C. cougar

   D. puma

   E. bear

8 **A.** azure

   B. cobalt

   C. emerald

   D. navy

   E. sapphire

9   **A.** malbec

     B. chardonnay

     C. burgundy

     D. shiraz

     E. pilsen

10   **A.** chamois

     B. gabardine

     C. calico

     D. twill

     E. denim

ANSWERS

① D. flower
② A. radish
③ E. grater
④ A. perguin
⑤ C. diamond

⑥ B. cab
⑦ E. bear
⑧ C. emerald
⑨ E. pilsen
⑩ A. chamois

SCORING

Award 16.5 points for each correct answer.

165 Genius
148–132 Gifted/Superior Intelligence
115 Higher Than Usual Intelligence
99 Average Intelligence
83 Low Average Intelligence
70 or below Very Low Intelligence

Recognizing Patterns II

In each of the following groups of words, select the word that is not like the others.

1. **A.** dictionary
   B. atlas
   C. almanac
   D. encyclopedia
   E. memoir

2. **A.** cup
   B. gill
   C. bushel
   D. firkin
   E. hogshead

3. **A.** courage
   B. security
   C. perseverance
   D. fortitude
   E. patience

4. **A.** plot
   B. table of contents
   C. index
   D. chapter
   E. cover

5. **A.** yam
   B. cucumber
   C. potato
   D. sunchoke
   E. shallot

6. **A.** whale
   B. dolphin
   C. porpoise
   D. tuna
   E. seal

7. **A.** breach
   B. break
   C. brooch
   D. fissure
   E. gap

8. **A.** conductor
   B. author
   C. ballerina
   D. engraver
   E. contractor

⑨ **A.** numeracy

B. empty set

C. cosine

D. radius

E. matrix

⑩ **A.** dig

B. pot shard

C. stratosphere

D. midden

E. in situ

ANSWERS

① E. memoir
② C. bushel
③ B. security
④ A. plot
⑤ B. cucumber

⑥ D. tuna
⑦ C. brooch
⑧ E. contractor
⑨ A. numeracy
⑩ C. stratosphere

SCORING

Award 16.5 points for each correct answer.

165 Genius
148–132 Gifted/Superior Intelligence
115 Higher Than Usual Intelligence
99 Average Intelligence
83 Low Average Intelligence
70 or below Very Low Intelligence

Recognizing Patterns III

In each of the following groups of words, select the word that is not like the others.

1 **A.** grape seed oil

    B. aloe

    C. lanolin

    D. glycerin

    E. astringent

2 **A.** stamen

    B. petal

    C. stem

    D. tannin

    E. stigma

3 **A.** cowardice

    B. anxiety

    C. jealousy

    D. rapaciousness

    E. vanity

4 **A.** eulogy

    B. doggerel

    C. haiku

    D. sonnet

    E. epic

5 **A.** equilateral

    B. isosceles

    C. obtuse

    D. acute

    E. hypotenuse

6 **A.** polenta

    B. faro

    C. barley

    D. quinoa

    E. wheat berries

7 **A.** balloon

    B. fixed rate

    C. adjustable rate

    D. reverse

    E. truth-in-lending

8 **A.** carnation

    B. cyan

    C. fuchsia

    D. magenta

    E. rose

9 A. awl

B. fabric shears

C. bias

D. mannequin

E. seam ripper

10 A. repel

B. retort

C. oppose

D. withstand

E. weather

ANSWERS

① E. astringent
② D. tannin
③ B. anxiety
④ A. eulogy
⑤ E. hypotenuse

⑥ A. polenta
⑦ E. truth-in-lending
⑧ B. cyan
⑨ C. bias
⑩ B. retort

SCORING

Award 16.5 points for each correct answer.

165 Genius
148–132 Gifted/Superior Intelligence
115 Higher Than Usual Intelligence
99 Average Intelligence
83 Low Average Intelligence
70 or below Very Low Intelligence

Recognizing Patterns IV

In each of the following groups of words, select the word that is not like the others.

1 **A.** antic

B. frivolous

C. exploit

D. eccentric

E. amusing

2 **A.** epistolary

B. bildungsroman

C. dime

D. Gothic

E. burlesque

3 **A.** festivals

B. mores

C. customs

D. traditions

E. practices

4 **A.** globe

B. sphere

C. orb

D. rotunda

E. ball

5 **A.** falchion

B. scimitar

C. gladius

D. foil

E. stiletto

6 **A.** apt

B. absorbed

C. apposite

D. appropriate

E. fitting

7 **A.** lilac

B. aubergine

C. lavender

D. vermilion

E. violet

8 **A.** intransigent

B. inflexible

C. insufferable

D. unyielding

E. uncompromising

⑨ **A.** cubist

   B. still life

   C. landscape

   D. genre

   E. portrait

⑩ **A.** guru

   B. mystic

   C. shaman

   D. yeti

   E. sage

ANSWERS

① C. exploit

② E. burlesque

③ A. festivals

④ D. rotunda

⑤ E. stiletto

⑥ B. absorbed

⑦ D. vermilion

⑧ C. insufferable

⑨ A. cubist

⑩ D. yeti

SCORING

Award 16.5 points for each correct answer.

165 Genius
148–132 Gifted/Superior Intelligence
115 Higher Than Usual Intelligence
99 Average Intelligence
83 Low Average Intelligence
70 or below Very Low Intelligence

Recognizing Patterns V

In each of the following groups of words, select the word that is not like the others.

1. **A.** evening
   B. cocktail
   C. prom
   D. bridesmaid
   E. vintage

2. **A.** chambermaid
   B. gardener
   C. butler
   D. valet
   E. footman

3. **A.** excoriate
   B. berate
   C. upbraid
   D. criticize
   E. exculpate

4. **A.** square
   B. plaza
   C. cube
   D. piazza
   E. quadrangle

5. **A.** fork
   B. junction
   C. intersection
   D. crossroads
   E. bypass

6. **A.** genius
   B. muse
   C. inspiration
   D. motivation
   E. stimulation

7. **A.** teal
   B. lemon
   C. mustard
   D. saffron
   E. gold

8. **A.** adolescent
   B. tot
   C. youth
   D. youngster
   E. teenager

⑨ **A.** souvenir

   B. keepsake

   C. memento mori

   D. trinket

   E. knickknack

⑩ **A.** reference

   B. checkout

   C. stacks

   D. narthex

   E. periodical room

ANSWERS

① E. vintage
② B. gardener
③ E. exculpate
④ C. cube
⑤ E. bypass

⑥ A. genius
⑦ A. teal
⑧ B. tot
⑨ C. memento mori
⑩ D. narthex

SCORING

Award 16.5 points for each correct answer.

165 Genius
148–132 Gifted/Superior Intelligence
115 Higher Than Usual Intelligence
99 Average Intelligence
83 Low Average Intelligence
70 or below Very Low Intelligence

CHAPTER 6

FILL IN THE MISSING LETTERS

Hollywood IQ Scores

There is a common perception that when it comes to intellectual achievement, Hollywood actors run the gamut from dumb to dumber. That's an unfair characterization. The breathtakingly beautiful Hedy Lamarr, for example, was also incredibly intelligent—she was the co-inventor of a spread spectrum technique used in wireless communication. Of course, not everyone in Hollywood rises to that level of brilliance, but there are plenty of highly intelligent actors and actresses.

James Woods, 180
Judy Holliday, 172
Dolph Lundgren,160
Quentin Tarantino, 160

Sharon Stone, 154
Jayne Mansfield, 149
Steve Martin, 142
Geena Davis, 140
Madonna, 140
Shakira, 140
Arnold Schwarzenegger, 135
Jodie Foster, actress, 132
Nicole Kidman, 132

✏ Fill In The Missing Letters I

Fill in the missing letters to create words associated with comedy.

1 ___ U ___ LE ___ QU ___

2 F ___ RC ___

3 ___ U ___ O ___

4 ___ ES ___ IN ___

5 C ___ OW ___ IN ___

6 ___ OS ___

7 S ___ A ___ S ___ IC ___

8 ___ A ___ S

9 P ___ EA ___ A ___ T ___ Y

10 ___ A ___ P ___ O ___

ANSWERS ·

SCORING ·

Award 16.5 points for each correct answer.

165 Genius
148–132 Gifted/Superior Intelligence
115 Higher Than Usual Intelligence
99 Average Intelligence
83 Low Average Intelligence
70 or below Very Low Intelligence

✏️ Fill In The Missing Letters II

Fill in the missing letters to create words associated with romance.

1 A ___ F ___ I ___

2 ___ A ___ S ___ O ___

3 A ___ FE ___ T ___ O ___

4 ___ E ___ O ___ I ___ N

5 Y ___ AR ___ IN ___

6 ___ E ___ D ___ R

7 A ___ O ___ O ___ S

8 ___ O ___ I ___ G

9 S ___ A ___ RY-E ___ E ___

10 A ___ D ___ N ___

ANSWERS ·

⑩ ARDENT

⑨ STARRY-EYED

⑧ LOVING

⑦ AMOROUS

⑥ TENDER

⑤ YEARNING

④ DEVOTION

③ AFFECTION

② PASSION

① AFFAIR

SCORING ·

Award 16.5 points for each correct answer.

165 Genius
148–132 Gifted/Superior Intelligence
115 Higher Than Usual Intelligence
99 Average Intelligence
83 Low Average Intelligence
70 or below Very Low Intelligence

Fill In The Missing Letters III

Fill in the missing letters to create words associated with innocence.

① I ___ E ___ P ___ R ___ E ___ C ___

② ___ I ___ T ___ E

③ P ___ R ___ T ___

④ ___ N ___ O ___ R ___ P ___

⑤ B ___ A ___ E ___ E ___ S

6 ___ O ___ D ___ E ___ S

7 C ___ I ___ D ___ I ___ E

8 ___ N ___ E ___ U ___ U ___

9 N ___ Ï ___ E

10 ___ R ___ S ___ I ___ G

A N S W E R S

10 TRUSTING
6 NAÏVE
8 INGENUOUS
7 CHILDLIKE
9 GOODNESS

5 BLAMELESS
4 INCORRUPT
3 PURITY
2 VIRTUE
1 INEXPERIENCE

S C O R I N G

Award 16.5 points for each correct answer.

165 Genius
148–132 Gifted/Superior Intelligence
115 Higher Than Usual Intelligence
99 Average Intelligence
83 Low Average Intelligence
70 or below Very Low Intelligence

✎ Fill In The Missing Letters IV

Fill in the missing letters to create words associated with work.

1 ___ O ___ L

2 R ___ P ___ T ___ T ___ O ___ S

3 ___ E ___ A ___ D ___ N ___

4 L ___ B ___ R

5 ___ O ___ A ___ I ___ N

6 O ___ C ___ P ___ T ___ O ___

7 ___ U ___ E ___ V ___ S ___ R

8 S ___ L ___ R ___

9 ___ E ___ E ___ I ___ S

10 U ___ I ___ N

ANSWERS ·

10 UNION

6 BENEFITS

8 SALARY

7 SUPERVISOR

9 OCCUPATION

5 VOCATION

4 LABOR

3 REWARDING

2 REPETITIOUS

1 TOIL

SCORING ·

Award 16.5 points for each correct answer.

165 Genius
148–132 Gifted/Superior Intelligence
115 Higher Than Usual Intelligence
99 Average Intelligence
83 Low Average Intelligence
70 or below Very Low Intelligence

✏️ Fill In The Missing Letters V

Fill in the missing letters to create words associated with entertainment.

1. A ___ U ___ E ___ E ___ T

2. ___ H ___ A ___ E ___

3. D ___ N ___ E

4. ___ O ___ I ___

5. P ___ A ___

6. ___ E ___ F ___ R ___ A ___ C ___

7. S ___ O ___

8. ___ A ___ D ___ V ___ L ___ E

9. A ___ P ___ A ___ S ___

10. ___ A ___ G ___ T ___ R

ANSWERS ·

⑩ LAUGHTER
⑨ APPLAUSE
⑧ VAUDEVILLE
⑦ SHOW
⑥ PERFORMANCE

⑤ PLAY
④ MOVIE
③ DANCE
② THEATER
① AMUSEMENT

SCORING ·

Award 16.5 points for each correct answer.

165 Genius
148–132 Gifted/Superior Intelligence
115 Higher Than Usual Intelligence
99 Average Intelligence
83 Low Average Intelligence
70 or below Very Low Intelligence

CHAPTER 7

THE RIGHT WORD

Mensa International

Have you heard of Mensa? It is an organization of people with impressively high IQ scores. To qualify for membership, your IQ score must be in the top 2 percent of the population. In other words, 98 percent of people who have taken an IQ test are not eligible to join Mensa.

The society was founded in 1946 by Lancelot Ware, a graduate student who was studying law at Oxford University, and Roland Berrill, an Australian barrister who hung around the university, although his application for admission to Oxford had been rejected. Initially they called their society the High IQ Club. The name did not have much panache, so Ware and Berrill considered changing it to Mens, the Latin term for mind. Unfortunately, Mens was also the name of a racy men's magazine. So they chose Mensa,

Latin for "table," because the organization was to be a round table where no one was judged on the basis of their background or belief system. (Ironically, Ware and Berrill learned later that in Mexican slang, mensa means idiot).

Mensa has about 110,000 members in 100 countries across the globe. And they're not all brain surgeons and Nobel Prize-winning physicists. Sure, there are professors and scientists who are members of Mensa, but there are also firefighters, musicians, farmers, police officers, truck drivers, and members of the military.

This diverse group of people doesn't just sit around trying to impress one another with how smart they are. Nor do they promote any particular political, religious, or social agenda. According to the Mensa website, the organization is committed to three goals:

1. "To identify and foster human intelligence for the benefit of humanity.
2. To encourage research in the nature, characteristics and uses of intelligence.
3. To promote stimulating intellectual and social opportunities for its members."

Mensa publishes a journal for its members that features articles on a wide range of topics. The organization also publishes a newsletter that spotlights special events and activities that may be of interest to Mensa members. There is also the *Mensa Research Journal*, published for non-members, which addresses the nature of human intelligence.

The Right Word I

Identify the word that fits the definitions.

1. A strand or fiber of material.

   F _____

2. To be important or well-known.

   P _____

3. Something that stands for or represents something else.

   S _____

4. To be happy or optimistic.

   C _____

5. In geometry, a four-sided figure with four angles.

   T _____

6. A nonstick coating often used for cookware.

   T _____

7. Money collected by a government from its citizens.

   T _____

8. An informal term for a dirty or disreputable tavern, bar, or restaurant.

   D _____

9. Squares of pasta filled, typically, with meat or cheese.

   R _____

10. A cold-blooded animal that lives on land and in the water, but breeds exclusively in water.

    A _____

ANSWERS

10. Amphibian
9. Ravioli
8. Dive
7. Tax
6. Teflon

5. Tetragon
4. Cheerful
3. Symbol
2. Prominent
1. Filament

SCORING

Award 16.5 points for each correct answer.

165 Genius
148–132 Gifted/Superior Intelligence
115 Higher Than Usual Intelligence
99 Average Intelligence
83 Low Average Intelligence
70 or below Very Low Intelligence

✏️ The Right Word II

Identify the word that fits the definitions.

1. An artifact, the remains of a building, or the remains of someone or something considered holy.

    R _____

2. The organ enclosed inside the cranium that controls the nervous system.

    B _____

3. An expert who leads groups of visitors around a tourist destination.

    D _____

4. A corm, tuber, or rhizome from which a flowering plant grows every year.

    B _____

5. A liquid, often thickened, served to enhance the flavor of meat, fish, vegetables, or other dishes.

S _____

6. To be well-spoken, but in an insincere way.

G _____

7. A person who has a condition that it makes it challenging to perform common tasks of daily life.

D _____

8. A mechanism typically found in rivers to raise or lower ships.

L _____

9. A hard, underwater organism, famous for its distinctive colors; often made into jewelry.

C _____

10. A small open-sided structure often found in gardens or other scenic locations.

G _____

ANSWERS

5. Sauce
4. Bulb
3. Docent
2. Brain
1. Relic

10. Gazebo
6. Coral
8. Lock
7. Disabled
9. Glib

SCORING

Award 16.5 points for each correct answer.

165 Genius
148–132 Gifted/Superior Intelligence
115 Higher Than Usual Intelligence
99 Average Intelligence
83 Low Average Intelligence
70 or below Very Low Intelligence

✏️ The Right Word III

Identify the word that fits the definitions.

1 A diplomat sent to a foreign nation to represent his or her nation's interests.

A _____

2 A crease in the skin or in fabric.

W _____

3 Kernels of a type of grain that puff up when heated.

P _____

4 A deer less than a year old.

F _____

5 Office machinery that destroys documents.

S _____

6 An edible, thin-skinned tuber, usually orange in color.

C _____

7 An athlete who works to increase the size of his or her muscles.

B _____

8 To be silly, unwise, or show a lack of judgment.

F _____

9 A violent emotion, usually in response to being insulted or offended.

A _____

10 A foreigner who settles in a new country.

I _____

ANSWERS ·

10 Immigrant
9 Anger
8 Foolish
7 Bodybuilder
9 Carrot

5 Shredder
4 Fawn
3 Popcorn
2 Wrinkle
1 Ambassador

S C O R I N G ·

Award 16.5 points for each correct answer.

165 Genius
148–132 Gifted/Superior Intelligence
115 Higher Than Usual Intelligence
99 Average Intelligence
83 Low Average Intelligence
70 or below Very Low Intelligence

The Right Word IV

Identify the word that fits the definitions.

1. Describing a wound that oozes pus.

   S _____

2. Criminal involved in organized crime.

   M _____

3. An alcoholic beverage made by fermenting grapes.

   W _____

4. To shake or tremble, often from cold or fear.

   S _____

5. The Sun and its planets, satellites, asteroids, meteors, and comets.

   S _____

6. The inability to make a decision. Also a breakfast pastry.

   W _____

7. The level of moisture in the atmosphere.

   H _____

8 A virtue that demonstrates sound judgment in making decisions in practical matters.

P _____

9 Something lethal or fatal.

D _____

10 To be kind and courteous.

G _____

ANSWERS

10 Gracious

9 Deadly

8 Prudence

7 Humidity

6 Waffle

5 Solar System

4 Shudder

3 Wine

2 Mobster

1 Septic

SCORING

Award 16.5 points for each correct answer.

165 Genius
148–132 Gifted/Superior Intelligence
115 Higher Than Usual Intelligence
99 Average Intelligence
83 Low Average Intelligence
70 or below Very Low Intelligence

The Right Word V

Identify the word that fits the definitions.

1 Someone who arranges romantic relationships intended to lead to marriage.

M _____

2 Water in its solid form.

I _____

3 An area covered with dense tropical vegetation.

J _____

4 Characteristic of being frugal.

E _____

5 To receive a guest or visitor happily.

W _____

6 Characteristic of someone who endures a delay or long wait or even a form of suffering without complaint.

P _____

7 A work of fiction with a long, complicated plot, usually involving many characters.

N _____

8 To be intelligent and creative in solving problems.

C _____

9 An enclosed area where spectators watch athletes.

S _____

10 A measure of someone's intelligence, based on a test score.

I _____

ANSWERS

① Matchmaker
② Ice
③ Jungle
④ Economical
⑤ Welcome
⑥ Patience
⑦ Novel
⑧ Clever
⑨ Stadium
⑩ IQ

SCORING

Award 16.5 points for each correct answer.

165 Genius
148–132 Gifted/Superior Intelligence
115 Higher Than Usual Intelligence
99 Average Intelligence
83 Low Average Intelligence
70 or below Very Low Intelligence

CHAPTER 8

WORD PAIRS

Famous Members of Mensa

Jean Auel is the author of the best-selling novels *Clan of the Cave Bear*, *Valley of Horses*, and *Plains of Passage*.

Richard Bolles' book, *What Color is Your Parachute?*, was *The New York Times* Bestseller List for 228 weeks.

Adrian Cronauer is a radio personality made famous in the movie *Good Morning Vietnam*.

Geena Davis is an Academy Award-winning actress who starred in *A League of Their Own* and *Thelma and Louise*.

Maurice Kanbar invented and owns Skyy Vodka.

Richard Lederer is a renowned "pun-master," has appeared often on National Public Radio. He is the author of numerous books on word play.

Harry Milligan is a boxer who won the 1983 National Amateur Heavyweight championship.

Ellen Morphonios is a former model and beauty queen who serves as a judge in Florida, where her strict rulings have earned her the nickname, "Maximum Morphonios."

Barry Nolan is co-anchor of the TV program *Hard Copy*.

Donald Petersen was chairman of the Ford Motor Company where he was involved in the development of the Mustang and the Maverick—two of Ford's most successful automobiles.

Julie Peterson is a chiropractor and former Playboy Playmate.

Marilyn Vos Savant is featured in the Guinness Hall of Fame for having the world's highest recorded IQ score—228. She writes the "Ask Marilyn" column in *Parade* magazine.

Linda Warwick created and produced the wildly popular Babymugs! and Toddler TOGS videos.

Deborah Yates dances with the Radio City Rockettes.

✏️ Word Pairs I

Pair one word from Column A with one word from Column B to create a common two-word expression. For example, Big + Top forms Big Top.

COLUMN A	COLUMN B
1 Well	Times
2 Left	Hearted
3 Thin	Mail
4 Warm	Movie
5 Cold	Face
6 Happy	Five
7 Express	Skinned
8 High	Day
9 Dirty	Fish
10 Hard	Heeled

ANSWERS ·

10 Hard Times
6 Dirty Movie
8 High Five
7 Express Mail
9 Happy Day

5 Cold Fish
4 Warm Hearted
3 Thin Skinned
2 Left Face
1 Well Heeled

SCORING ·

Award 16.5 points for each correct answer.

165 Genius
148–132 Gifted/Superior Intelligence

115 Higher Than Usual Intelligence
99 Average Intelligence
83 Low Average Intelligence
70 or below Very Low Intelligence

Word Pairs II

Pair one word from Column A with one word from Column B to create a common two-word expression. For example, Big + Top forms Big Top.

COLUMN A	COLUMN B
1 Never	Kennel
2 Every	Cream
3 Pickup	Show
4 Wake-up	Mind
5 Puppet	Fountain
6 Dog	Call
7 Doll	Chocolate
8 Soda	Truck
9 Ice	Day
10 Hot	Hospital

ANSWERS

10 Hot Chocolate
9 Ice Cream
8 Soda Fountain
7 Doll Hospital
6 Dog Kennel

5 Puppet Show
4 Wake-up Call
3 Pickup Truck
2 Every Day
1 Never Mind

SCORING ·····························

Award 16.5 points for each correct answer.

165 Genius
148–132 Gifted/Superior Intelligence
115 Higher Than Usual Intelligence
99 Average Intelligence
83 Low Average Intelligence
70 or below Very Low Intelligence

Word Pairs III

Pair one word from Column A with one word from Column B to create a common two-word expression. For example, Big + Top forms Big Top.

COLUMN A	COLUMN B
1 Movie	Scan
2 Thumb	Crumbs
3 Fig	Court
4 Independent	Teller
5 Pocket	Pot
6 Brain	Star
7 Flower	Watch
8 Bread	Tack
9 Basketball	Leaf
10 Bank	Contractor

ANSWERS

① Movie Star
② Thumb Tack
③ Fig Leaf
④ Independent Contractor
⑤ Pocket Watch
⑥ Brain Scan
⑦ Flower Pot
⑧ Bread Crumbs
⑨ Basketball Court
⑩ Bank Teller

SCORING

Award 16.5 points for each correct answer.

165 Genius
148–132 Gifted/Superior Intelligence
115 Higher Than Usual Intelligence
99 Average Intelligence
83 Low Average Intelligence
70 or below Very Low Intelligence

✏️ Word Pairs IV

Pair one word from Column A with one word from Column B to create a common two-word expression. For example, Big + Top forms Big Top.

COLUMN A

1. Gregorian
2. Gold
3. Character
4. Living
5. Lay
6. Sitting
7. Prop
8. Fried
9. Public
10. Bar

COLUMN B

Plane
Color
Exam
Standard
Chicken
Television
Chant
Claim
Pretty
Assassination

ANSWERS ·

10. Bar Exam
9. Public Television
8. Fried Chicken
7. Prop Plane
6. Sitting Pretty

5. Lay Claim
4. Living Color
3. Character Assassination
2. Gold Standard
1. Gregorian Chant

SCORING ·

Award 16.5 points for each correct answer.

165 Genius
148–132 Gifted/Superior Intelligence

115 Higher Than Usual Intelligence
99 Average Intelligence
83 Low Average Intelligence
70 or below Very Low Intelligence

Word Pairs V

Pair one word from Column A with one word from Column B to create a common two-word expression. For example, Big + Top forms Big Top.

COLUMN A	COLUMN B
1 Bar	Body
2 Public	Temperature
3 Best	Off
4 Merry	Start
5 Love	Pepper
6 Hands	Man
7 Head	Widow
8 Bell	Affair
9 Student	None
10 Daytime	Enemy

ANSWERS

1 Bar None
2 Public Enemy
3 Best Man
4 Merry Widow
5 Love Affair
6 Hands Off
7 Head Start
8 Bell Pepper
9 Student Body
10 Daytime Temperature

SCORING ·

Award 16.5 points for each correct answer.

165 Genius
148–132 Gifted/Superior Intelligence
115 Higher Than Usual Intelligence
99 Average Intelligence
83 Low Average Intelligence
70 or below Very Low Intelligence

CHAPTER 9

ENGLISH IDIOMS

The Origins of the SAT Test

Carl Brigham, an American psychologist, invented the Scholastic Aptitude Test (SAT) in the late 1890s to eliminate a common problem in college admissions department—bias against applicants based on their race, ethnicity, religion, or economic background. The first test was given in 1901 to 973 students. The test asked very specific questions on such subjects as English, French, German, Latin Greek, history, chemistry, and physics. For example, this question came from the Latin section of the 1901 test:

Write the rules for the following constructions and illustrate each by a Latin sentence:

A. Two uses of the dative.
B. The cases used to indicate the relations of place.
C. The cases used with verbs of remembering.
D. The hortatory (or jussive) subjunctive.
E. The supine in um.

By 1926 the SAT had evolved into an examination that tested logical thinking and reading comprehension rather than specific knowledge. It was still very demanding—test-takers were given only 90 minutes to answer 315 questions. The SAT has continued to change over the years; in 2005, for example, the Math section was made harder in response to the rising number of test takers who were getting 800—a perfect score.

Like the IQ test, the SAT has its share of critics. In California, a study found that students whose family had an annual income of $20,000 or less on average scored 1310 (out of a possible 1600), while students whose family had an income of $200,000 or more scored on average 1715. Critics found evidence of cultural bias in the questions. For example, students were asked to complete the analogy, "Runner is to marathon as oarsman is to. . . ." The correct answer is "regatta," a reference to the sport of crew. A study found that 53 percent of white students answered that question correctly, but only 22 percent of black students. In response to these critics, many colleges no longer require the SAT as part of the admissions process.

✏ English Idioms I

English idiomatic expressions often pair two words to express a single idea; for example, *dead and gone* to convey that someone is deceased. Fill in the missing word or words in the following pairs.

1 _____ and drakes

2 a gentleman and _____ _____

3 all bark and _____ _____

4 _____ _____ and no steak

5 _____ and beyond

6 an arm and _____ _____

7 _____ and battery

8 bag and _____

9 _____ _____ and sevens

10 _____ and bull

A N S W E R S

1 ducks and drakes
2 a gentleman and a scholar
3 all bark and no bite
4 all sizzle and no steak
5 above and beyond
6 at sixes and sevens
7 assault and battery
8 bag and baggage
9 an arm and a leg
10 cock and bull

SCORING ....

Award 16.5 points for each correct answer.

165 Genius
148–132 Gifted/Superior Intelligence
115 Higher Than Usual Intelligence
99 Average Intelligence
83 Low Average Intelligence
70 or below Very Low Intelligence

✏ English Idioms II

English idiomatic expressions often pair two words to express a single idea; for example, *dead and gone* to convey that someone is deceased. Fill in the missing word or words in the following pairs.

1 _____ and call

2 high and _____

3 between a rock and _____ _____ _____

4 _____ and fancy free

5 between Scylla and _____

6 _____ and mean

7 _____ _____ and end all

8 _____ and whistles

9 dribs and _____

10 neck and _____

ANSWERS

① beck and call
② high and mighty
③ between a rock and a hard place
④ footloose and fancy free
⑤ between Scylla and Charybdis
⑥ dribs and drabs
⑦ be all and end all
⑧ bells and whistles
⑨ lean and mean
⑩ neck and neck

SCORING

Award 16.5 points for each correct answer.

165 Genius
148–132 Gifted/Superior Intelligence
115 Higher Than Usual Intelligence
99 Average Intelligence
83 Low Average Intelligence
70 or below Very Low Intelligence

✏ English Idioms III

English idiomatic expressions often pair two words to express a single idea; for example, *dead and gone* to convey that someone is deceased. Fill in the missing word or words in the following pairs.

1 _____ and bothered

2 blood and _____

3 _____ and needles

4 _____ and balances

5 chapter and _____

6 _____ and dried

7 crash and _____

8 dog and _____ _____

9 _____ and gloom

10 birds and _____

ANSWERS

1 hot and bothered
2 blood and guts
3 pins and needles
4 checks and balances
5 chapter and verse
6 doom and gloom
7 crash and burn
8 dog and pony show
9 cut and dried
10 birds and bees

SCORING

Award 16.5 points for each correct answer.

165 Genius
148–132 Gifted/Superior Intelligence
115 Higher Than Usual Intelligence
99 Average Intelligence
83 Low Average Intelligence
70 or below Very Low Intelligence

✏ English Idioms IV

English idiomatic expressions often pair two words to express a single idea; for example, *dead and gone* to convey that someone is deceased. Fill in the missing word or words in the following pairs.

1 _____ _____ _____ and the deep blue sea

2 fits and _____

3 _____ and center

4 _____ and go

5 hard and _____

6 _____ and blue

7 here and _____

8 _____ and outs

9 kit and _____

10 _____ and between

ANSWERS ·

5 hard and fast

4 grab and go

3 front and center

2 fits and starts

1 between the devil and the deep blue sea

10 betwixt and between

9 kit and caboodle

8 ins and outs

7 here and now

9 black and blue

SCORING ·

Award 16.5 points for each correct answer.

165 Genius
148–132 Gifted/Superior Intelligence
115 Higher Than Usual Intelligence
99 Average Intelligence
83 Low Average Intelligence
70 or below Very Low Intelligence

English Idioms V

English idiomatic expressions often pair two words to express a single idea; for example, *dead and gone* to convey that someone is deceased. Fill in the missing word or words in the following pairs.

1 meat and _____

2 _____ and oranges

3 _____ and cranny

4 _____ and dime

5 born and _____

6 once and _____ _____

7 _____ and parcel

8 _____ _____ and pound foolish

9 _____ and tumble

10 _____ and save

ANSWERS

① meat and potatoes
② apples and oranges
③ nook and cranny
④ nickel and dime
⑤ born and bred

⑥ rough and tumble
⑦ part and parcel
⑧ penny wise and pound foolish
⑨ once and for all
⑩ scrimp and save

SCORING

Award 16.5 points for each correct answer.

165 Genius
148–132 Gifted/Superior Intelligence
115 Higher Than Usual Intelligence
99 Average Intelligence
83 Low Average Intelligence
70 or below Very Low Intelligence

CHAPTER 10

CORRECT THE MISSPELLED WORDS

SAT Scores of the Rich and Famous

These SAT scores are easy to find online, but no one can say with any certainty if they are accurate. We reproduce them here purely for entertainment value.

Paul Allen, co-founder of Microsoft, 1600

Bill Gates, co-founder of Microsoft, 1590

Bill O'Reilly, journalist, author, social and political commentator, 1585

James Woods, actor, 1579

Ben Stein, actor, writer, political commentator, 1573

Rush Limbaugh, radio personality and social
and political commentator, 1530

Al Gore, former vice president of the United States, 1355

George W. Bush, former president of the United States, 1206

Courtney Cox, actress, 1150

Amy Tan, author, 1110

Kobe Bryant, basketball star, 1080

Bill Clinton, former president of the United States, 1032

Al Franken, comedian, U.S. senator, 1020

✏ Correct the Misspelled Words I

Each of the following words is misspelled. Spell each word correctly.

1 phalsetto

_____

6 harrass

_____

2 accomodate

_____

7 decieve

_____

3 destinashun

_____

8 enfranchize

_____

4 acolyght

_____

9 civilizaytion

_____

5 cantancerous

_____

10 sibilante

_____

ANSWERS ·

10 sibilant

9 civilization

8 enfranchise

7 deceive

6 harass

5 cantankerous

4 acolyte

3 destination

2 accommodate

1 falsetto

SCORING ·····································

Award 16.5 points for each correct answer.

165 Genius
148–132 Gifted/Superior Intelligence
115 Higher Than Usual Intelligence
99 Average Intelligence
83 Low Average Intelligence
70 or below Very Low Intelligence

✏ Correct the Misspelled Words II

Each of the following words is misspelled. Spell each word correctly.

1 seege

2 catalist

3 respectible

4 verminus

5 akaline

6 embarass

7 voyour

8 delikacy

9 centriphigal

10 grammarion

ANSWERS ·

⑩ grammarian

⑨ centrifugal

⑧ delicacy

⑦ voyeur

⑥ embarrass

⑤ alkaline

④ verminous

③ respectable

② catalyst

① siege

SCORING ·

Award 16.5 points for each correct answer.

165 Genius
148–132 Gifted/Superior Intelligence
115 Higher Than Usual Intelligence
99 Average Intelligence
83 Low Average Intelligence
70 or below Very Low Intelligence

✏ Correct the Misspelled Words III

Each of the following words is misspelled. Spell each word correctly.

① newstand

_____

② crapulus

_____

③ sarcofagus

_____

④ vermichelli

_____

⑤ propertyed

_____

⑥ fortifys

_____

7 crannial

_____

9 locomoshun

_____

8 scaberous

_____

10 sinequre

_____

ANSWERS ·

10 sinecure

9 locomotion

8 scabrous

7 cranial

6 fortifies

5 propertied

4 vermicelli

3 sarcophagus

2 crapulous

1 newsstand

SCORING ·

Award 16.5 points for each correct answer.

165 Genius
148–132 Gifted/Superior Intelligence
115 Higher Than Usual Intelligence
99 Average Intelligence
83 Low Average Intelligence
70 or below Very Low Intelligence

✏️ Correct the Misspelled Words IV

Each of the following words is misspelled. Spell each word correctly.

1 mysticue

_____

2 harmmonium

_____

3 burlezque

_____

4 institutionel

_____

5 quandarry

_____

6 quary

_____

7 querey

_____

8 perilus

_____

9 phantastical

_____

10 ballisticks

_____

ANSWERS ·

10 ballistics

9 fantastical

8 perilous

7 query

6 quarry

5 quandary

4 institutional

3 burlesque

2 harmonium

1 mystique

SCORING . . . .

Award 16.5 points for each correct answer.

165 Genius
148–132 Gifted/Superior Intelligence
115 Higher Than Usual Intelligence
99 Average Intelligence
83 Low Average Intelligence
70 or below Very Low Intelligence

✏ Correct the Misspelled Words V

Each of the following words is misspelled. Spell each word correctly.

1 blith

    _____

2 reminicent

    _____

3 voraycious

    _____

4 whiste

    _____

5 tremulos

    _____

6 harbinnger

    _____

7 victuial

    _____

8 hummungous

    _____

9 relikuary

    _____

10 sinonim

    _____

ANSWERS

(10) synonym

(9) reliquary

(8) humungous

(7) victual

(6) harbinger

(5) tremulous

(4) whistle

(3) voracious

(2) reminiscent

(1) blithe

SCORING

Award 16.5 points for each correct answer.

165 Genius
148–132 Gifted/Superior Intelligence
115 Higher Than Usual Intelligence
99 Average Intelligence
83 Low Average Intelligence
70 or below Very Low Intelligence

UNSCRAMBLE
THE LETTERS

The LSAT

Frank Bowles, an admissions officer at the Columbia University Law School in New York City created the Law School Aptitude Test (LSAT) in 1945 as a reliable way to gauge the suitability of law school applicants. Until 1945, almost every law school in the United States had relied primarily on the grade point average of applicants. Bowles invited admission officers from other major law schools to work with him in developing a prototype. Representatives from Harvard and Yale signed on, however the admissions officers at New York University were sceptical that such a test would serve any purpose. But by 1947 other law schools were working with Bowles and his colleagues, and the first LSAT was administered in 1948. Today the test is offered four times a year to prospective law school applicants.

The test measures reading comprehension, logical reasoning, analytical reasoning, and requires a writing sample. A perfect score is 180, and such a score is extremely rare.

Since 1998, Michael Nieswiadomy, an economist at the University of North Texas, has conducted several studies which attempt predict the college majors of law school applicants who do best on the LSAT. He studied LSAT test scores by major and found . . .

UNDERGRADUATE MAJOR	AVERAGE SCORE
1. Mathematics/Physics	160
2. Economics and Philosophy/Theology	157.4
3. International Relations	156.5
4. Engineering	156.2
5. Government service and Chemistry	156.1
6. History and Interdisciplinary studies	155.5
7. Foreign languages	155.3
8. English	155.2
9. Biology/Natural sciences	154.8
10. Arts	154.2

What do the scores mean? The Ivy League law schools, as well as top-tier law schools such as Stanford, generally require scores of 160 or above. Scores in the 159-150 range may gain the applicant admission to a state university law school. Applicants who score below 150 will probably have trouble gaining admission to a law school.

Unscramble the Letters I

Unscramble the letters to create an English word or name.

1 talictan

   A. Atlantis

   B. athletic

   C. autism

   D. Atlantic

2 recrog

   A. retro

   B. grocer

   C. gawker

   D. Oscar

3 thilezabe

   A. Elizabeth

   B. errand

   C. errant

   D. barrage

4 xnvie

   A. vicious

   B. vixen

   C. never

   D. Nineveh

5 lydarceptt

   A. Pericles

   B. lethargic

   C. pterodactyl

   D. pictogram

6 calios

   A. social

   B. solar

   C. calico

   D. solicit

7 quasashuenn

   A. seaquake

   B. succotash

   C. suspenseful

   D. Susquehanna

8 delif

   A. fled

   B. flies

   C. delight

   D. field

9 revnima

    A. monetary

    B. moument

    C. Minerva

    D. marvelous

10 krabey

    A. crabby

    B. bakery

    C. kraken

    D. bicker

ANSWERS

① D. Atlantic
② B. grocer
③ A. Elizabeth
④ B. vixen
⑤ C. pterodactyl
⑥ A. social
⑦ D. Susquehanna
⑧ D. field
⑨ C. Minerva
⑩ B. bakery

SCORING

Award 16.5 points for each correct answer.

165 Genius
148–132 Gifted/Superior Intelligence
115 Higher Than Usual Intelligence
99 Average Intelligence
83 Low Average Intelligence
70 or below Very Low Intelligence

✏ Unscramble the Letters II

Unscramble the letters to create an English word or name.

1 eenurve

    A. renovate

    B. revenue

    C. revive

    D. nervous

2 sriragon

    A. garrison

    B. dragon

    C. garnish

    D. garish

3 giacoch

    A. jester

    B. Chicago

    C. gigantic

    D. cherish

4 stivior

    A. visor

    B. Swedish

    C. visitor

    D. variant

5 tryucen

    A. censure

    B. century

    C. triplicate

    D. triangle

6 clanhios

    A. Nicholas

    B. cholera

    C. churlish

    D. nascent

7 iusceni

    A. cousin

    B. cuisine

    C. scenery

    D. squish

8 slaitoe

    A. salivate

    B. icicles

    C. cuisine

    D. isolate

9 theckin

    A. thickens

    B. chicken

    C. check-in

    D. kitchen

10 rateric

    A. erratic

    B. rated

    C. terrific

    D. exotic

A N S W E R S ·

1. B. revenue
2. A. garrison
3. B. Chicago
4. C. visitor
5. B. century

6. A. Nicholas
7. B. cuisine
8. D. isolate
9. D. kitchen
10. A. erratic

S C O R I N G ·

Award 16.5 points for each correct answer.

165 Genius
148–132 Gifted/Superior Intelligence
115 Higher Than Usual Intelligence
99 Average Intelligence
83 Low Average Intelligence
70 or below Very Low Intelligence